Copyright © 2024 by Jason Brown

All rights reserved. No part of this publication may be reproduced, distributed, or transmitted in any form or by any means, including photocopying, recording, or other electronic or mechanical methods, without the prior written permission of the publisher, except in the case of brief quotations embodied in critical reviews and certain other non-commercial uses permitted by copyright law.

ISBN 979-8-9917469-1-5

First Edition: October, 2024

For permission requests, please contact Jason Brown at venturespherellc@gmail.com.

Book design by Esther Knox-Dekoning

Printed in the United States.

ART FABRO · DODGERS · 1952 · TOPPS

CHAS BENDER · ATHLETICS · 1911 · AMERICAN TOBACCO CO.

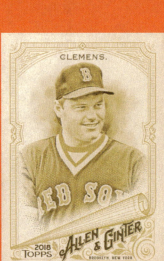
ROGER CLEMENS · RED SOX · 2018 · ALLEN & GINTER

BABE RUTH · NY YANKEES · 1933 · GOUDEY

FOR ALL SPORTS CARD
COLLECTORS - OLD AND NEW

UNLOCK THE SECRETS OF COLLECTING AND SELLING SPORTS CARDS

Illustrated and designed by Esther Knox-Dekoning

VENTURE SPHERE LLC

CONTENTS

I.
UNDERSTANDING SPORTS CARD COLLECTING
12

The SCORE Method — 16
The Basics of Sports Card Collecting — 18
Factors that Determine Sports Card Value — 20

II.
BUILDING YOUR SPORTS CARD COLLECTION
23

Tips for Finding Rare and Valuable Sports Cards — 25
Organizing and Displaying Your Sports Card Collection — 26

III.
SELLING YOUR SPORTS CARDS
30

Pricing and Negotiating Strategies for Selling Sports Cards — 33
Platforms for Selling Sports Cards Online — 33

IV. INVESTING IN SPORTS CARDS 39

Identifying Investment-Worthy Sports Cards 43
Long-Term Strategies for Maximizing Returns 44

V. AVOIDING COMMON PITFALLS 47

Mistakes to Avoid in Sports Card Collecting and Selling 49
How to Spot Fake Sports Cards 52

VI. WRAPPING IT UP 55

Summary 56
Resources for Further Learning and Exploration 57
Key Checklists 60

Notes 62
Index 66
Acknowledgements 69
About the Author 70

I.
UNDERSTANDING SPORTS CARD COLLECTING

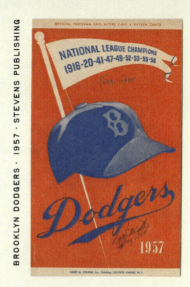

Sports card collecting is an exciting hobby that involves acquiring and preserving trading cards featuring athletes from various sports.

Understanding the dynamics of sports card collecting is key to building confidence. Engaging with other collectors through forums and local clubs not only enhances the experience but also provides valuable insights. Staying informed about market trends and participating in events further boosts both your confidence and the value of your collection.

By equipping yourself with this knowledge, you can step confidently into the world of sports card collecting. Happy collecting!

Most collectors start by focusing on a specific sport or player they are passionate about, which helps keep the hobby enjoyable and manageable. Key essentials include proper storage, such as a binder with protective sleeves, and a checklist to track your collected cards.

SEVERAL FACTORS DETERMINE THE VALUE OF SPORTS CARDS: RARITY, CONDITION, AND PLAYER POPULARITY.

Rare cards, particularly limited-edition or rookie cards, often hold significant value. A card's condition, evaluated using a grading system, needs to be pristine for top valuation. Finally, the popularity of the featured athlete can greatly influence a card's worth.

I'd like to introduce the SCORE methodology, a useful approach to assess and enhance your collection!

FIG 01

Embark on an exciting journey of sports card collecting with a structured plan using the SCORE method. This simple and effective guide will ensure you build a valuable and well-maintained collection.

S

STUDY.

Begin by immersing yourself in the world of sports and its players. Research the history, key statistics, and current trends. Understanding the nuances of different sports and the value of players' cards will provide you with a solid foundation to build upon.

COLLECT.

Once you've done your research, start acquiring cards. Visit local card shops, browse online auctions, and attend sports memorabilia shows. Keep an eye out for rare finds and good deals to strategically expand your collection.

ORGANIZE.

As your collection grows, maintaining order becomes essential. Use a spreadsheet to log important details about each card, such as the player, year, condition, and value. This organization will help you track your collection effectively and make it easier to manage.

R E

RETAIN.

Preservation is key to maintaining your cards' value. Invest in quality storage solutions, including card sleeves, toploaders, and binders. Proper storage protects your cards from damage and deterioration, ensuring they remain in excellent condition.

EVALUATE.

Regularly assess and update your collection. Stay informed about market trends and periodically re-evaluate the value and condition of your cards. This habit ensures that your collection remains both valuable and well-maintained.

THE BASICS OF SPORTS CARD COLLECTING

Starting this hobby requires clear steps and focus. Begin by choosing a specific sport or athlete of interest, which makes the experience more manageable and enjoyable. Investing in basic supplies is essential. Binders, protective sleeves, and storage boxes help keep your cards in top condition.

RESEARCH IS CRITICAL

Understanding the history and popularity of certain cards provides a solid foundation. Beginners should visit local card shops, attend sports memorabilia shows, and join online forums to gain valuable insights and discover potential finds.

CREATE AN ACTION PLAN TO STREAMLINE THE PROCESS

Start with a research phase. Study the sport, notable players, and significant card sets using reliable sources like sports card guides and online databases. Keep a checklist to track cards you want and those you've already acquired.

ACQUISITION COMES AFTER RESEARCH

Begin by purchasing affordable options to build your confidence. Buy both online and offline from reputable dealers to avoid counterfeits. Auction sites and trading groups can also offer opportunities for unique finds.

ORGANIZATION KEEPS COLLECTIONS PRISTINE

Maintain a detailed spreadsheet that logs card condition, acquisition date, and value estimates. Regularly update this record to track your progress and any increases in value.

PRESERVATION IS CRUCIAL

Quality storage solutions, such as acid-free sleeves and sturdy binders, protect your cards from damage. Avoid exposure to extreme temperatures and humidity, and store your collection in a cool, dry place.

VINTAGE TICKET OFFICE SIGN

CLAYTON KERSHAW · LA DODGERS · 2008 · TOPPS

FACTORS THAT DETERMINE SPORTS CARD VALUE

Understanding the elements that influence a sports card's value is crucial for collectors. The first and most important factor is condition. Cards in mint condition command the highest prices, with assessment criteria including centering, corners, edges, and surfaces. Using a grading service, such as PSA or Beckett, provides an objective evaluation.

Rarity also significantly impacts value. Limited edition cards or those from short print runs tend to be more valuable. Collectors should research the print runs of various sets and identify scarce cards. Templates for tracking such details can help keep things organized.

Player popularity is another major determinant. Cards of well-known or Hall of Fame athletes are often in high demand. Monitoring player performance and trends in the sports world can help predict shifts in card value.

The age and historical significance of a card also matter. Vintage cards, especially those from the early 20th century, often hold substantial value. However, even modern cards can be valuable if they commemorate significant milestones or events. Creating a timeline or historical tracker can assist in identifying key cards worth acquiring.

Brand and set influence a card's worth, too. Popular brands like Topps, Upper Deck, and Panini produce highly regarded sets. Tracking industry trends and understanding the reputation of different brands can guide informed purchasing decisions.

Finally, authenticity is paramount. Ensuring that cards are genuine is crucial for avoiding losses. Always acquire cards from reputable sources and use authenticity verification services. Keeping a record of authenticity for each card enhances confidence in the collection.
By systematically addressing these factors, collectors can make informed decisions and build a valuable collection. Templates and action plans for

condition assessment, rarity tracking, and authenticity verification can streamline the process.

ORGANIZATION IS KEY TO A ROBUST COLLECTION.
Sort cards by categories such as team, player, and year. Use acid-free sleeves and binders to preserve card condition. Digital spreadsheets or specialized software can track inventory and value, simplifying cataloging.

DISPLAYING THE COLLECTION ENHANCES BOTH ENJOYMENT AND VALUE.
Invest in quality display cases or wall frames with UV protection. Rotating the display frequently minimizes light exposure and potential damage. Label displays with relevant card details for easy identification.

TEMPLATES AND ACTION PLANS STREAMLINE THE COLLECTING PROCESS.
Create a wish list template to prioritize acquisitions. Develop a budget plan to manage spending effectively. Checklist templates ensure all collection goals are met systematically.

REGULARLY REVIEW AND UPDATE THE COLLECTION STRATEGY.
Market conditions and player performance change, affecting card values. Adapting the strategy ensures the collection remains relevant and valuable.

By following these guidelines, collectors can confidently build a purposeful and valuable sports card collection.

FIG 02

II.

BUILDING YOUR SPORTS CARD COLLECTION

A successful sports card collection begins with strategic planning. Start by focusing on a specific sport, player, or era. This narrows the scope and makes the collection more manageable. Utilize online databases and collector forums to research market trends and values.

Finding rare and valuable sports cards requires diligence. Attend local and online auctions, join collector groups, and frequent card shows. Utilize search functions on marketplaces like eBay to track specific cards. Establish relationships with reputable dealers for insider tips.

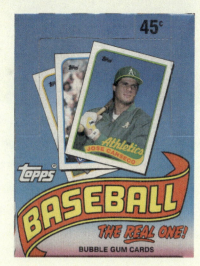

TIPS FOR FINDING RARE AND VALUABLE SPORTS CARDS

Finding rare and valuable sports cards requires a strategic approach. Start by researching current market trends and identifying in-demand cards using resources like online databases, collector forums, and price guides. These tools can help you understand what makes a card valuable.

Participation in auctions is highly recommended, as both local and online auctions present opportunities to acquire rare cards. Platforms like eBay allow users to set alerts for specific cards, ensuring collectors never miss a valuable listing.

Joining collector groups and clubs can be immensely beneficial. Networking with other collectors provides tips and exclusive access to rare finds. Being part of a community also offers support and a shared pool of collective knowledge.

Regularly attending card shows is another effective strategy. These events often feature a variety of dealers who may have the rare cards you're seeking. Negotiating in person can sometimes yield better deals than online purchases.

To streamline the search, use a wish list template that lists desired cards with details such as player name, year, and estimated value. Having this information readily available helps you stay focused during your searches.

Finally, building relationships with reputable dealers is crucial. Trusted dealers can provide advanced knowledge about upcoming sales and new inventory. Often, these relationships lead to insider tips that aren't available to the general public.

By following these guidelines, collectors can maximize their chances of finding rare and valuable sports cards effectively..

ORGANIZING AND DISPLAYING YOUR SPORTS CARD COLLECTION

Organizing and displaying a sports card collection requires careful planning. Start by sorting the cards into categories such as sport, player, team, or year. Using a sorting tray can help speed up this process.

Invest in protective supplies to keep your cards safe. Card sleeves and toploaders provide essential protection from damage, while magnetic holders are ideal for securing high-value cards. Store the cards in a sturdy box or binder with labeled dividers for easy access and organization.

I.
CATEGORIZE YOUR CARDS BY SPORT, PLAYER, TEAM, OR YEAR
Organize the collection by sorting the cards into categories for easier management and display.

II.
INVEST IN PROTECTIVE SUPPLIES
Use card sleeves, toploaders, or magnetic holders for high-value cards to keep them safe from damage.

III.
CREATE AN INVENTORY LIST
Maintain a detailed list that includes information like card condition, acquisition date, and estimated value. This helps track the collection's growth and value over time.

IV.
CHOOSE A DEDICATED SPACE FREE FROM DIRECT SUNLIGHT
Select a storage area that avoids exposure to direct sunlight to prevent fading and damage.

V.
SET ASIDE TIME EACH WEEK TO ORGANIZE AND UPDATE THE COLLECTION
Regularly review and update the inventory to ensure everything remains in order and properly documented.

CREATE AN INVENTORY LIST

Use a spreadsheet or inventory management app to log each card's details, such as player name, year, and condition. This step is essential for tracking your collection and assessing its value. Templates for inventory lists are available online to simplify this task.

CHOOSE A DEDICATED SPACE FOR DISPLAY

Select an area free from direct sunlight to prevent fading. Display cases with UV protection are ideal for preserving your cards. Arrange them by theme or player for a visually appealing setup, and consider framing high-value cards individually for a striking presentation.

IMPLEMENT AN ACTION PLAN FOR EFFICIENCY

Set aside time each week to organize and update your collection. Dedicate specific time slots for inventory updates, cleaning, and refreshing the display. This routine helps keep your collection in optimal condition.

STAY CONNECTED WITH THE COLLECTOR COMMUNITY

Join forums and attend card shows to exchange tips and gain insights on maintaining and displaying collections effectively. Engaging with other collectors can provide valuable knowledge and opportunities.

Following this structured approach to organizing and displaying your sports card collection ensures optimal protection while professionally showcasing the cards. A well-organized collection not only looks impressive but also makes it easier to manage and enjoy.

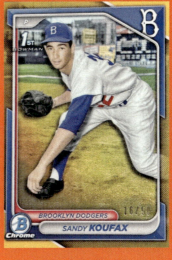

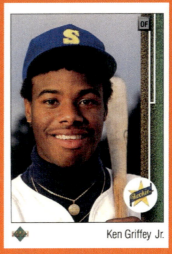

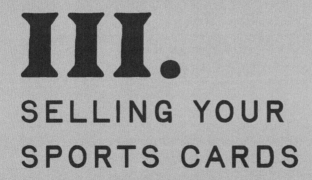

III.
SELLING YOUR SPORTS CARDS

FIG 03

Selecting the right platform is crucial for successful sports card trading. eBay is a popular choice, offering options for both auctions and fixed-price listings.

For quicker sales, consider COMC (Check Out My Cards), which handles shipping and provides a streamlined selling process.

Social media platforms like Facebook groups and Instagram also offer trading opportunities, allowing for direct interactions with potential buyers. Be sure to research each platform's fees and policies before committing to ensure it aligns with your selling goals.

PRICING AND NEGOTIATING STRATEGIES FOR SELLING SPORTS CARDS

Accurate pricing is crucial when selling sports cards. Begin by researching recent sales of similar cards on platforms like eBay to gauge market value. Tools such as the Beckett Price Guide can provide additional insights. Always take the card's condition into account—cards in better condition typically command higher prices.

When listing cards, use high-quality images and provide detailed descriptions to attract buyers. Highlight any special features, such as autographs or limited editions. Ensure the correct spelling of the player's name and other details to reach your target audience effectively.

Negotiation is a key part of the selling process. Be prepared to counter offers and set a minimum price beforehand to avoid underselling. During negotiations, use your gathered data to justify your asking price and support your position.

Use templates for listing cards that maintain a consistent format for descriptions, pricing, and shipping details. An action plan for maximizing sales should include regularly monitoring market trends, adjusting prices accordingly, and maintaining clear communication with potential buyers.

By following these steps, sellers can approach transactions with confidence and increase the likelihood of a successful sale.

PLATFORMS FOR SELLING SPORTS CARDS ONLINE

Choosing the right platform to sell sports cards can significantly affect the success of your transactions. For beginners, eBay is a user-friendly option that offers both auction-style listings and fixed-price sales. With a large user base, it provides extensive reach for sellers.

COMC (Check Out My Cards) offers a more streamlined process, handling

EXAMPLE

2022 TOPPS CHROME MIKE TROUT AUTOGRAPHED CARD

Mint condition, sharp corners, authenticated signature, and includes original packaging.

US $250
open to reasonable offers

Ships within two business days with tracking.

storage, scanning, and shipping for sellers. This platform allows you to focus on pricing and marketing, making it ideal for those looking to offload large collections without dealing with logistics.

Social media platforms like Facebook feature specialized groups where collectors buy, sell, and trade cards. For a more personalized approach, Instagram allows sellers to showcase high-quality images and interact directly with potential buyers, fostering a sense of community and trust.

Using templates to create uniform listings ensures consistency. Include sections for the card's brand, player name, year, condition, and special attributes like autographs to make listings comprehensive.

An action plan should involve regular market analysis to adjust listings based on current trends. Tools such as the Beckett Price Guide and recent eBay sales figures can guide pricing decisions. Additionally, maintaining clear communication through prompt responses to inquiries helps build buyer confidence.

Accurate pricing is essential. Start by researching recent sales of similar cards on platforms like eBay, and use the Beckett Price Guide as a reference. Monitoring these sources helps establish a reliable baseline value.

When setting prices, take card conditions into account. Cards in mint condition typically command higher prices. Be sure to highlight any special attributes, such as autographs, rookie status, or limited editions. Being transparent about the card's condition can attract serious buyers.

Decide whether to use fixed prices or auctions. Fixed prices offer control and predictability, while auctions can generate excitement and potentially drive prices higher.

In negotiations, be prepared to justify your asking price by emphasizing the card's unique features and citing recent sales of comparable items. It's important to remain flexible; offering a slight discount may close a sale and encourage repeat business. Follow up with potential buyers who haven't committed, and politely remind them of the card's value and benefits. Building rapport can increase the chances of a transaction.

These strategies, combined with templates and action plans, can streamline the pricing and negotiation process. This approach ensures competitive and fair pricing, smooth negotiations, and a higher likelihood of successful sales.

When negotiating, be prepared to justify the asking price. Highlight the card's unique features and recent sales of comparable items. It's crucial to remain flexible. Offering a slight discount might close a sale and foster repeat business. Follow up with potential buyers who haven't committed. Politely remind them of the card's value and benefits. Building rapport increases the chances of a transaction.

These strategies, templates, and action plans can streamline the pricing and negotiation. This approach ensures competitive, fair pricing and smooth negotiations, increasing the likelihood of successful sales.

ACTION PLAN FOR NEGOTIATION:

SET CLEAR PRICE RANGES

Establish a price range for each card

Determine the Minimum Acceptable Price: The lowest amount you're willing to accept.

Note your Ideal Selling Price: The target amount you aim to achieve.

RESPOND PROMPTLY

Answer buyer inquiries quickly to maintain interest and build trust.

USE DATA

Cite recent sale prices to justify your asking price and support negotiations.

FIG 04

IV.
INVESTING IN SPORTS CARDS

Investing in sports cards can be a lucrative venture, but the key is identifying cards with strong potential for appreciation.

Start by focusing on players with promising careers ahead. Consider investing in rookies or young stars who are making headlines. Begin by researching current market trends using platforms like eBay and Beckett, which offer valuable insights. Review past sales to identify patterns in player performance and card price changes.

Building a diversified collection is essential. Invest in cards from different sports and eras to mitigate risk and maximize potential returns. Diversification helps balance the portfolio and reduces exposure to fluctuations in any single market segment.

Long-term investment strategies often involve holding onto cards until they reach peak value. Patience is crucial in this approach. Regularly reassess your portfolio and adjust holdings based on market dynamics and emerging trends.

By following these strategies and using the provided templates, investors can build a profitable sports card portfolio with confidence. Remember, knowledge and patience are key to long-term success in this field.

TEMPLATE FOR IDENTIFYING INVESTMENT-WORTHY SPORTS CARDS:

Player Name: (e.g., Zion Williamson)
Card Type: (e.g., Rookie Card)
Condition: (e.g., Mint/ Near Mint)
Attributes: (e.g., Autographed, Limited Edition)

ACTION PLAN FOR DIVERSIFIED INVESTMENT:

Set a Budget: Determine how much to invest in total and per card.
Research Thoroughly: Study player statistics and card history.
Buy from Reputable Sources: Ensure authenticity and proper grading.
Track Market Trends: Keep up with news and updates in the sports card market.

REGULAR PORTFOLIO MAINTENANCE:

Quarterly Review: Evaluate card values and adjust if necessary.
Condition Check: Ensure cards remain in optimal condition for maximum value.
Market Analysis: Stay updated with sports news relevant to your investments.

TEMPLATE FOR EVALUATING A SPORTS CARD

CARD CONDITION:

○ Near mint or better: Comparable to a fresh pack
○ Excellent: Has clearly visible signs of wear
○ Very good: Has moderate-to-heavy damage all over
○ Poor: Is extremely worn and displays flaws all over

CONDITION TYPE:

○ Graded: Professionally graded
○ Ungraded: Not in original packaging or professionally graded

INSET OPTIONS:

○ Base Set   ○ Chase   ○ Digital
○ Insert   ○ Memorabilia   ○ Parallel/Variety

AUTOGRAPH FORMATS:

○ Hard Signed ○ Cut   ○ Label or Sticker

ADDITIONAL IDENTIFIES

○ Season   ○ Manufacturer   ○ Features
○ Set   ○ Team   ○ Parallel/Variety

IDENTIFYING INVESTMENT-WORTHY SPORTS CARDS

Investing in sports cards requires keen judgment and thorough research. The first step is to identify players with strong career prospects. Rookies or emerging stars often make promising investments, and tracking player performance and industry news can offer valuable insights.

Next, focus on card types. Rookie cards typically hold higher value, especially for players who go on to achieve success. Specialized cards, such as autographed or limited editions, also present lucrative opportunities for investors.

Understanding the card's condition is vital. Cards in Mint or Near Mint condition fetch premium prices. To ensure authenticity and quality, aim to acquire cards that have been professionally graded.

Source cards from reputable sellers. Platforms like eBay and Beckett provide market insights and reliable transactions, but always check a seller's reviews and ratings before making a purchase.

Patience is essential. Hold onto valuable cards until their market value peaks. Regularly monitor the sports card market and adjust your investments based on current trends.

By following these guidelines, investors can confidently identify and capitalize on investment-worthy sports cards.

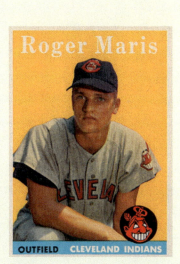

ROGER MARIS · INDIANS · 1958 · TOPPS

LONG-TERM STRATEGIES FOR MAXIMIZING RETURNS

Successful sports card investing relies on a solid long-term strategy. Start with thorough research and stay informed about players, market trends, and shifts. Focus on monitoring key players, particularly rookies and emerging talents who have the potential to reach significant career milestones.

Diversify your portfolio to mitigate risk. Invest in a mix of high-profile and lesser-known players across different sports. This approach balances potential gains and reduces exposure to the performance of any single player.

Quality over quantity is essential. Prioritize acquiring cards in Mint or Near Mint condition. Professionally graded cards are preferred, as they ensure authenticity and help preserve value. Networking with other collectors and investors can also provide valuable insights and help you spot opportunities early.

ACTION PLAN FOR INVESTMENT:

Research: Analyze player statistics and future potential.
Buy Strategically: Focus on rookie cards and high-quality conditions.
Verify Authenticity: Purchase from trusted platforms and check for grading certifications.
Diversify: Build a collection across different players and sports to spread risk.

SET CLEAR GOALS:
• Define your investment objectives and establish specific timeframes.
• Set a budget for acquiring new cards, ensuring it aligns with your overall strategy.

REGULAR MARKET REVIEW:
• Review card prices and market trends on a quarterly basis.
• Adjust your holdings based on player performance and changing market conditions.

SECURE STORAGE:
• Use protective cases and climate-controlled environments to preserve card condition.
• Prevent damage by ensuring proper storage and handling.

Patience is essential in sports card investing. Avoid impulsive sales and hold onto cards until significant career milestones or market peaks are reached.

Stay updated with industry publications, forums, and social media groups. Online platforms like eBay, Beckett, and PSA forums offer valuable market insights.

Consider consulting with seasoned collectors and investors to refine your strategies. Collaboration can lead to better decision-making and improved returns. By following these steps, investors can maximize returns and build a profitable sports card portfolio.

CHECKLIST FOR MONITORING INVESTMENTS:

Quarterly Reviews: Assess card value changes.
Condition Maintenance: Ensure cards remain in top condition.
Market Tracking: Stay updated with relevant sports news.

FIG 05

V.
AVOIDING COMMON PITFALLS

Understanding how to spot fake sports cards is crucial for collectors. Start by familiarizing yourself with known counterfeits, as organizations like PSA and Beckett offer resources and lists of commonly faked cards.

Carefully inspect the card's print quality, checking for clear text and sharp images. Fake cards often show signs of poor print quality, such as blurred edges or inconsistent coloring. Additionally, verify card details against official databases, paying close attention to player statistics and team affiliations. Inconsistencies in these details can be a red flag.

OHTANI, TROUT, PUJOLS · ANGELS · 2020 · TOPPS

MISTAKES TO AVOID IN SPORTS CARD COLLECTING AND SELLING

Beginners often make avoidable mistakes when it comes to sports card collecting. One common error is improper storage. Poor storage can degrade card quality, significantly reducing its value. Always use protective sleeves and keep cards in climate-controlled environments to maintain their condition.

Another pitfall is neglecting market trends. It's important to stay updated on player performances and market shifts to make informed buying and selling decisions. Avoid making emotional trades based on short-term events; patience and thorough research tend to yield better long-term results.

One of the biggest mistakes collectors make is neglecting research. Understanding the market is crucial, including recognizing established trends and identifying undervalued cards.

With these guidelines, collectors can avoid common pitfalls, ensuring a more successful and enjoyable experience in sports card collecting and selling.

RESEARCH ACTION PLAN:
- Dedicate time daily for market research to stay updated on trends and values.
- Utilize tools like eBay's completed listings to track recent sales and price trends.
- Follow industry experts on social media for insights and updates.

Not protecting your cards can lead to devaluation. Ensure they are stored in appropriate sleeves and cases, and avoid exposure to direct sunlight and humidity.

PROTECTION CHECKLIST:
- Purchase acid-free sleeves for safe storage.
- Use hard plastic toploaders to provide extra protection.
- Store cards in a climate-controlled environment to prevent damage.

Avoid overpaying for cards, a common mistake for new collectors. Always compare prices across multiple sellers before making a purchase.

PRICE COMPARISON TEMPLATE:
- List the top three online marketplaces for comparison.
- Note the prices for the desired card on each platform.
- Average the prices to determine a fair market value.

Ignoring professional grading can severely impact potential resale value. Grading provides assurance of authenticity and condition, boosting buyer confidence.

GRADING ACTION PLAN
- Research reputable grading services such as PSA and Beckett.
- Submit valuable cards for professional grading.
- Keep detailed records of all submissions and results for future reference.

Impulse buying, driven by emotions rather than strategy, often leads to regret. Develop a clear plan before attending card shows or browsing online.

IMPULSE CONTROL TIPS:
- Set a budget and commit to it.
- Create a list of target cards before attending events or shopping online.

ACTION PLAN FOR
IDENTIFYING FAKE SPORTS CARDS

RESEARCH & DOCUMENTATION

- Bookmark reputable anti-counterfeit resources and study common counterfeit indicators.
- Stay informed about the latest trends in fake sports cards to recognize potential red flags.

CARD INSPECTION ROUTINE

- Use magnification tools to examine the card's print quality, edges, and details.
- Compare the card with authenticated versions to spot any inconsistencies.

DATABASE VERIFICATION

- Cross-check player stats and card information against official sports card registries.
- Use trusted databases to verify card authenticity and details.

Selling at the wrong time can lead to financial loss. Understanding optimal selling times, often linked to player performance and market conditions, can help maximize returns.

SELLING TIMING STRATEGY:
- Monitor player performance statistics closely.
- Stay updated on market trends.
- Time sales to coincide with peak interest in the player.

By adhering to these guidelines, collectors can avoid common pitfalls and build a more successful and enjoyable sports card collection.

HOW TO SPOT FAKE SPORTS CARDS

Recognizing fake sports cards is essential for collectors. Start by familiarizing yourself with known counterfeits using resources from PSA and Beckett. Study the print quality of genuine cards; authentic cards feature crisp images and clear text, while fakes often appear blurry.

MISTAKE-AVOIDANCE TEMPLATE:

Storage Checklist:
- Use acid-free sleeves and magnetic-hard cases.
- Maintain optimal temperature and humidity.

Market Research Schedule:
- Set monthly alerts for player news.
- Review quarterly market reports.

Trading Discipline Rules:
- Establish a no-impulse trade rule.
- Have a review period before finalizing sales.

PRINT QUALITY CHECKLIST:
- Examine text sharpness.
- Check for image clarity.

Next, inspect the card's cardstock. Genuine cards have a specific weight and texture, while counterfeit cards may feel lighter or excessively glossy. Whenever possible, compare the suspected fake to an authenticated card.

CARDSTOCK COMPARISON STEPS:
- Hold both cards side by side.
- Note any differences in texture, weight, and gloss.

Additionally, verify details such as player stats. Cross-check information with official sports card registries, as discrepancies may indicate a fake.

VERIFICATION TEMPLATE:
- Look up player stats in an official registry.
- Match all details with the card in question.

Modern cards may include hidden security features that can be revealed under UV light. This check helps confirm if the card meets authentication standards.

SECURITY FEATURES SCAN:
- Shine UV light on the card.
- Identify any hidden marks or patterns.

Lastly, consider professional appraisals for high-value cards. Reputable grading services can provide a definitive assessment of authenticity.

APPRAISAL ACTION PLAN:
- Submit the card to a recognized grading service (e.g., PSA or Beckett).
- Review the certification and assessment results.

By following these steps and using tools like print quality checklists and database verifications, collectors can confidently identify and avoid fake sports cards.

FIG 06

The key to a successful sports card journey is staying informed and systematic. Regular research should become a habit. That way, collectors can build both knowledge and confidence.

Firstly, consistent research is invaluable. Dedicate at least 15 minutes daily to market study, using tools like eBay's completed listings to track prices. Following industry experts and participating in community forums will keep you informed and help you make better decisions.

Protecting your cards is also an essential step. Use high-quality acid-free sleeves, hard plastic toploaders, and store them in climate-controlled environments. Create a protection checklist to ensure your cards are kept away from sunlight and humidity, preserving their condition and value. Compare prices across multiple marketplaces to find fair value. Use a price comparison template by identifying the top three marketplaces, documenting prices, and averaging them to determine a fair buying price.

Finally, grading is also important for serious collectors. Utilize reputable services like PSA or Beckett to authenticate and grade high-value cards. Maintain detailed submission logs to track your graded cards. A grading action plan should include accurately evaluating results to prepare for effective listing.

Additionally, avoid impulse buys by setting a strict budget and creating a list of target cards before purchasing events. This approach helps safeguard your investments and ensures thoughtful acquisitions.

By following these systematic strategies, collectors can confidently navigate the market, achieving both enjoyment and financial success.

RESOURCES FOR FURTHER LEARNING AND EXPLORATION

For those new to sports card collecting, reliable resources are essential. Several tools and strategies can help collectors and sellers on their journey.

BEGIN WITH DEDICATED ONLINE FORUMS

Websites like Sports Card Forum or 133Point offer valuable information. Engage in discussions, ask questions, and learn from the experiences of other collectors.

CONSIDER SUBSCRIBING TO INDUSTRY MAGAZINES

Publications such as Sports Collectors Digest and Beckett Magazine provide insights into trends and market values. Bookmarking key articles can serve as quick reference points.

PODCASTS ARE ANOTHER EXCELLENT RESOURCE

Shows like Sports Cards Nonsense and Sports Card Investor cover various aspects of the hobby.

UTILIZING SOCIAL MEDIA IS CRUCIAL

Platforms like Instagram and Twitter feature many well-known collectors and dealers who share their knowledge. Following hashtags like #sportscards and #cardcollecting will keep you updated on the latest trends.

FOR THOSE INCLINED TOWARDS STRUCTURED LEARNING, CONSIDER ONLINE COURSES

Some websites can offer informative models on sports and non-sports card collecting. An effective action plan would be to research to ensure the course meets your needs and level of understanding.

MAINTAIN A DIGITAL JOURNAL

Keeping a digital journal to log valuable information and key learnings can be invaluable. Consider creating a template with sections for card condition, market trends, expert tips, and personal notes to keep everything organized.

LOCAL CARD SHOWS AND MEETUPS OFFER HANDS-ON EXPERIENCE

Attending these events provides opportunities to network and observe the nuances of card trading firsthand.

By utilizing these resources diligently, collectors and sellers can enhance their expertise and make informed decisions.

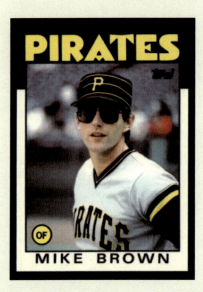

MIKE BROWN · PIRATES · 1986 · TOPPS

WRAPPINGN IT UP

FIG 07

KEY CHECKLISTS

RESEARCH ACTION PLAN:

◯ Dedicate 15 minutes daily to market research.

◯ Use tools like eBay's completed listings for price tracking.

◯ Follow industry experts and forums.

Proper storage is essential for maintaining card value. Use acid-free sleeves and hard plastic toploaders, and store your collection in a climate-controlled environment to prevent degradation.

PROTECTION CHECKLIST:

◯ Buy high-quality sleeves and cases.

◯ Opt for climate-controlled storage.

◯ Keep cards away from sunlight and humidity.

Compare prices across multiple platforms before buying to ensure you're getting fair value. Be vigilant for overpricing and always aim for the best deal.

PRICE COMPARISON TEMPLATE:

- ◯ Identify three top marketplaces.
- ◯ Compare and document prices.
- ◯ Determine an average to find a fair buying price.

Grading enhances credibility and boosts resale value. Choose reputable services like PSA or Beckett, and keep detailed records of all submissions.

GRADING ACTION PLAN:

- ◯ Submit high-value cards for grading.
- ◯ Maintain detailed submission logs.
- ◯ Evaluate grading results for accurate listings.

Develop a budget and adhere to it. Monitor performance stats and market trends to determine the optimal times to sell, maximizing your profits.

IMPULSE CONTROL PLAN:

- ◯ Set a strict budget.
- ◯ List target cards before any purchasing event.

By following these checklists, collectors can confidently navigate the sports card market, ensuring both enjoyment and financial success.

NOTES:

NOTES:

NOTES:

NOTES:

WORKS CITED

All photos and cards used throughout this publication have been sourced from publicly available online platforms. We have made every effort to credit the original creators, and links to the sources are provided in the index. If any discrepancies or unintentional oversights are found, please contact us for appropriate attribution or removal.

IMAGES

Inside Cover — The Dibs Team. (2022). *The 6 Best Places to Buy & Sell Baseball Cards Online* [Photograph]. Dibbs. https://dibbs.io/blog/sell-baseball-cards-online

Fig 01 — Alano, E. (2024). *How to sell sports card collection?* [Photograph]. Fan Arch. https://fanarch.com/blogs/sports-cards/how-to-sell-sports-card-collection

Fig 02 — JB Hobby Sports Cards & Collectibles. *1970s Topps Baseball Sports Card Collection Yankees Mets Cubs Royals Orioles* [Photograph]. eBay. https://www.ebay.com/itm/116302600736

Fig 03 — AP Photo/Jeff Chiu. (2020). *Have some old baseball cards? Here's what to know before you try to sell* [Photograph]. News Nation. https://www.newsnationnow.com/us-news/sports/have-some-old-baseball-cards-heres-what-to-know-before-you-try-to-sell/

Fig 04 — Koeppel, J. (2021). *The 20 Most Valuable Baseball Cards of All-Time* [Photograph]. ONE37pm, Editors. https://www.one37pm.com/popular-culture/most-valuable-baseball-cards

Fig 05 — Memorabilia Expert. (2021). *Sports Card Rack Pack Collection Lot 1982 & 1984 Topps Football, 1985 Baseball* [Photograph]. Memorabilia Expert. https://www.memorabilia.expert/shop/sports-card-rack-pack-collection-lot-1982-1984-topps-football-1985-baseball/

Fig 06 — @user2260163650. (2021). *Lot A various baseball cards* [Photograph]. Mercari. https://www.mercari.com/us/item/m80513894503/

Fig 07 — *PSA 10 2018 Topps Shohei Ohtani Chase* [Photograph]. eBay.

CITATIONS

American Tobacco Company. *Bender, Chas T205.* 1911.

Goudey Gum Co. *Ruth, Babe: Goudey #53.* 1933.

Lionel Carter Collection. *Mungo, Van: #26.* 1934.

ONE37pm Editors. "The Past, Present and Future of the Sports Card Industry." *ONE37pm*, 29 July 2019, www.one37pm.com/popular-culture/sports-cards-guide.

TOPPS. *Brown, Mike: TOPPS #114.* 1986.

---. *Checklist: TOPPS Baseball First Series Checklist.* 1957.
---. *Clemens, Roger: Allen and Ginter #233.* 2015.
---. *Fabro, Art #114.* 1952.
---. *Kershaw, Clayton: Allen & Ginter #72.* 2008.
---. *Koufax, Sandy: Bowman Chrome BCP-254.* 2024.
---. *Mantle, Mickey: TOPPS #311.* 1949.
---. *Maris, Roger: TOPPS #47.* 1958.
---. *Mattingly, Don: TOPPS #8.* 1982.
---. *Pignatano and Roseboro: TOPPS #292.* 1962.
---. *Pujols, Albert; Ohtani, Shohei; Trout, Mike: Triple Threads Auto Relic /9.* 2020.
---. *Ripken, Cal: TOPPS #98T.* 1982.
---. *Skenes, Paul: Bowman Draft #BD14.* 2022.
---. *Snider, Duke: TOPPS #32.* 1954.
---. *Various Cards: 1970's Assortment.*
---. *Various Cards: 1988 TOPPS Rack Packs.* 1985.

Upper Deck. *Griffey Jr., Ken: Upper Deck #1.* 1986.

ACKNOWLEDGEMENTS

First and foremost, to my amazing wife and daughter—thank you for putting up with all the card talk, stacks of memorabilia around the house, and the occasional "accidental" card purchases. You two are my greatest treasures, and your love and support mean the world to me.

To my dad—thank you for sharing your love of baseball with me, from watching games together to those hours spent discussing stats and legendary players. And to my mom and dad, thank you for buying me baseball cards growing up. You probably had no idea you were fueling a lifelong obsession, but hey, it's too late now!

To my brother—thanks for all the random packs of cards you left lying around. Those unexpected little discoveries of commons and curiosities definitely helped build the collection (even if you didn't know it at the time).

A huge shoutout to my neighbor Phil, who let me dive into his decades-old treasure trove of cards. I'm pretty sure I spent a ton of my childhood in his closet-turned-collector's den, wide-eyed and in awe.

Finally, a big thank you to all the local card shops I've visited over the years. You've been my second home, my treasure hunt grounds, and my favorite escape. Keep the wax packs coming!

JASON BROWN · 1991

TRADER™

JASON BROWN · 2024

ABOUT THE AUTHOR

Jason is a passionate baseball card collector who has turned a lifelong hobby into a way of connecting with fellow collectors and enthusiasts. With a desire to help grow the hobby of collecting, Jason designed the SCORE Method (Study, Collect, Organize, Retain, Evaluate), which helps collectors, young and old, build more meaningful collections. With years of experience in the sports memorabilia space, Jason enjoys sharing insights, tips, and strategies to help new and veteran collectors maximize the value and enjoyment of their collections.

From tracking down rare finds to diving deep into the game's history, Jason's passion for baseball cards is about more than just the cards themselves—it's about preserving the stories and memories behind each one. Whether discussing iconic rookie cards or finding hidden gems at local card shops for his personal collection, Jason brings a thoughtful and engaging perspective to the collecting community. He also treasures the time spent with his wife, daughter, and family, often sharing his love for the hobby with them.

In addition to card collecting, Jason is an entrepreneur and advocate for mental health through his work with Kutoa Project, a trauma-informed care organization serving East Africa. Kutoa Project provides counseling and youth programs focused on mental health, using evidence-based practices to support those affected by anxiety, depression, and trauma.
When not immersed in the world of sports cards or working to expand mental health services, Jason also leads the Ohio Valley Premier League (OVPL), one of the United States' largest regional amateur soccer leagues.

No matter the endeavor, Jason is driven by a passion for storytelling, community, and making a positive impact.

Made in the USA
Middletown, DE
08 November 2024